FOOD LISTOGRAPHY

MY DELICIOUS LIFE IN LISTS

CREATED BY LISA NOLA

ILLUSTRATIONS BY CLAUDIA PEARSON

CHRONICLE BOOKS
SAN FRANCISCO

ISBN 978-1-4521-4264-7

Manufactured in China

Illustrations by Claudia Pearson

Chronicle Books publishes distinctive books and gifts. From award-winning
children's titles, bestselling cookbooks, and eclectic pop culture to acclaimed
works of art and design, stationery, and journals, we craft publishing that's
instantly recognizable for its spirit and creativity. Enjoy our publishing and
become part of our community at www.chroniclebooks.com.

10 9 8 7 6 5 4 3 2 1

Chronicle Books LLC
680 Second Street
San Francisco, CA 94107
www.chroniclebooks.com

DEDICATED TO MY BEST FRIEND AND DOG TOKI
WHO NEVER MET A FOOD HE DIDN'T LIKE

IF I WERE A FLAVOR OR A SPICE,
I WOULD BE _____.

"ONE CANNOT THINK WELL, LOVE WELL,
SLEEP WELL, IF ONE HAS NOT DINED WELL."
—VIRGINIA WOOLF, *A ROOM OF ONE'S OWN*

IN THE REALM OF HUMAN EXPERIENCE, THE ENDLESS VARIETY OF
FLAVORS, AROMAS, AND TEXTURES WE ENCOUNTER THROUGH
FOOD IS A TRUE GIFT. FOOD CONNECTS US, NOURISHES US,
LEADS US ON ADVENTURES AND SOMETIMES INTO ECSTASY! AND
COOKING IS ONE OF HUMANKIND'S MOST CREATIVE ENDEAVORS,
THE RESULTS OF WHICH WE EXPERIENCE TOGETHER IN FAMILY
KITCHENS, BY CANDLELIGHT AT A RESTAURANT, OR LAYING BACK
ON A PICNIC BLANKET. WITH FOOD, WE CREATE UNIQUE MEMORIES
THAT BECOME PART OF OUR STORY . . . PART OF OUR LISTOGRAPHY.
FOOD LISTOGRAPHY IS FOR FOODIES, COOKS, GASTRONOMISTS,
AND ALL THOSE WHO NOTICE AND APPRECIATE THE DETAILS OF
WHAT THEY EAT.

THIS BOOK IS FOR RECORDING YOUR DINING AND CULINARY
ADVENTURES—PAST, PRESENT, AND ALL THAT ARE YET TO COME!
MAY YOU HAVE GOOD HEALTH, DELICIOUS FOODS, AND GREAT
CONVERSATION!

LISA NOLA
WWW.LISTOGRAPHY.COM

FOODS AND DISHES I DISLIKE

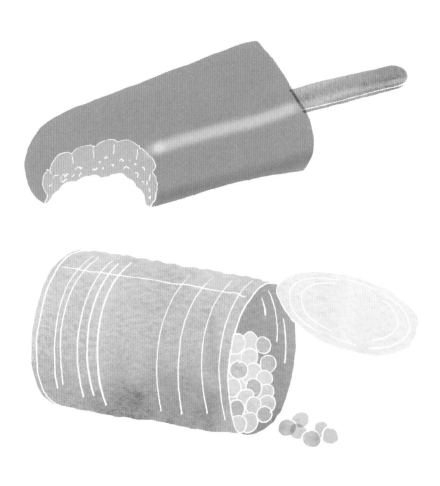

FUDGE POPS AND CANNED PEAS

MEMORABLE CHILDHOOD FOODS

GREEK FOOD

INTERNATIONAL CUISINES

I'VE TRIED

WANT TO TRY

MOROCCAN TAGINE, NORTH AFRICA

INTERNATIONAL DISHES

FAVORITE

WANT TO TRY

LABASSIN WATERFALL RESTAURANT, PHILIPPINES

RESTAURANTS ABROAD

FAVORITE

WANT TO TRY

A NEW ORLEANS' BEIGNET

CITY SPECIALTIES TO TRY

	CITY	SPECIALTY
☐		
☐		
☐		
☐		
☐		
☐		
☐		
☐		
☐		
☐		
☐		
☐		
☐		
☐		
☐		
☐		
☐		
☐		
☐		
☐		

CURRY IN A HURRY

MY LOCAL RESTAURANT HAUNTS

BARK-FEST CAFÉ (ALWAYS DOG-FRIENDLY)

BRUNCH RESTAURANTS

FAVORITE

WANT TO TRY

ITHAA UNDERSEA RESTAURANT, MAGICAL

RESTAURANTS I LOVE FOR THE AMBIENCE

RESTAURANT   AMBIENCE

VIRGINIA'S BY THE BEACH, ANNIVERSARY

MY SPECIAL OCCASION RESTAURANTS

RESTAURANT   OCCASION

CANTER'S DELI, LOS ANGELES

PLACES I'VE EATEN PAST MIDNIGHT

CHAIN RESTAURANTS I'VE BEEN TO

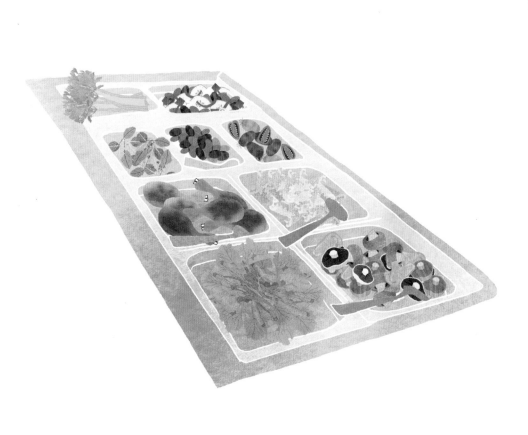

PLACES I'VE EATEN BUFFET-STYLE

BEST

WORST

MEDIEVAL TIMES

THEME RESTAURANTS AND DINNER THEATERS

I'VE DINED   WANT TO DINE

FANCY RESTAURANTS

I'VE DINED   WANT TO DINE

SUKI'S TACOS, CLOSED APRIL, 2010

SAD RESTAURANT CLOSINGS

WHEN THE MUSIC IS TOO LOUD

RESTAURANT PET PEEVES

THE LONGEST SERVICE WAIT, PARIS, 2000

WORST DINING EXPERIENCES

COOKING EGGS WHILE CAMPING IN YOSEMITE

MEMORABLE PICNIC AND OUTDOOR
EATING EXPERIENCES

Turmeric

Cinnamon

Dill

HERBS, SPICES, AND FLAVORS

FAVORITE

LEAST FAVORITE

Vanilla

Blueberry Glaze

Lavender

Sugar Rose

Honey Lemon

Maple Syrup with
marshmallow graham
cracker

CRONUTS

TRENDY FOODS AND DRINKS

I'VE TRIED   WANT TO TRY

A FUGU "PUFFER FISH"

STRANGE FOODS AND DRINKS

I'VE TRIED   WANT TO TRY

_____ ☐ _____

_____ ☐ _____

_____ ☐ _____

_____ ☐ _____

_____ ☐ _____

_____ ☐ _____

_____ ☐ _____

_____ ☐ _____

_____ ☐ _____

_____ ☐ _____

_____ ☐ _____

_____ ☐ _____

_____ ☐ _____

_____ ☐ _____

_____ ☐ _____

_____ ☐ _____

_____ ☐ _____

_____ ☐ _____

_____ ☐ _____

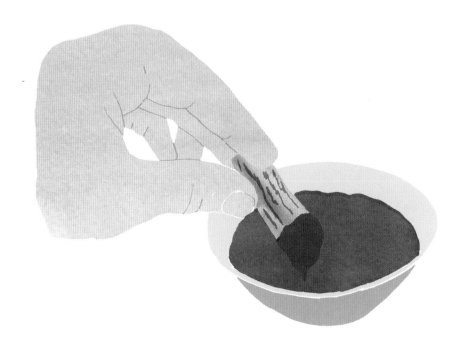

BACON CHOCOLATE

ODDEST FOOD COMBINATIONS
I'VE COME ACROSS

KALE, KALE, AND MORE KALE

FOODS FOR MY HEALTH

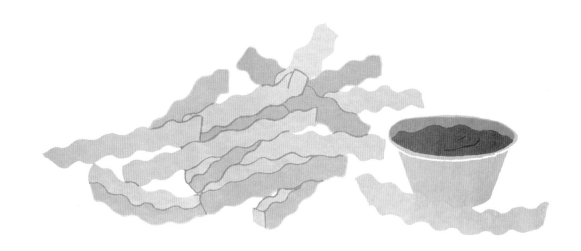

FRENCH FRIES AND KETCHUP

MY GUILTY PLEASURE FOODS

CHEESE & CRACKER LADYBUGS

YUMMY APPETIZERS

Cherry Tomatoes

Radish

Radicchio

Nuts

Chives

Salad

French Dressing

Spring Onions

FAVORITE SALAD INGREDIENTS

Epoisses

Stilton

Chevre

Parmigiano

Gorgonzola

Swiss

Camembert

CHEESES I'VE TRIED

ALPHABET SOUP

SOUPS AND STEWS

FAVORITE

WANT TO TRY

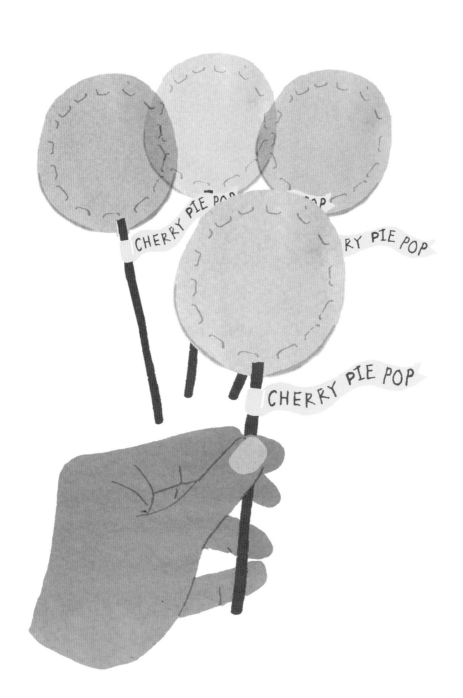

DESSERTS

FAVORITE   WANT TO TRY

☐

GINGERBREAD HOUSE, CHRISTMAS

HOLIDAY FOODS

FAVORITE

LEAST FAVORITE

FRUITS AND VEGETABLES

FAVORITE

LEAST FAVORITE

MERCADO VER-O-PESO, BELÉM, BRAZIL

FARMERS' MARKETS

I'VE BEEN TO

WANT TO VISIT

BAKERIES AND SWEET SHOPS

FAVORITE   WANT TO VISIT

CAFÉS AND TEA SHOPS

FAVORITE

WANT TO TRY

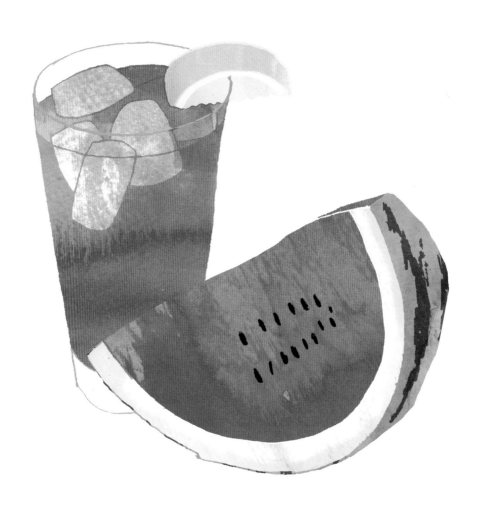

WATERMELON LEMONADE

BEVERAGES

FAVORITE

LEAST FAVORITE

BARS AND PUBS

FAVORITE

WANT TO TRY

THE SWEDISH CHEF, *SESAME STREET*

CHEFS

I LOVE

TO EXPLORE

□

LET'S EAT CUPCAKES COOKBOOK

COOKBOOKS, MAGAZINES, AND CULINARY RESOURCES

I LOVE

TO EXPLORE

THAI COOKING CLASS

COOKING CLASSES

I'VE TAKEN   WANT TO TAKE

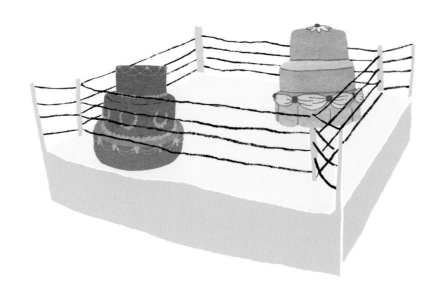

CAKE VS. CAKE

BEST COOKING SHOWS

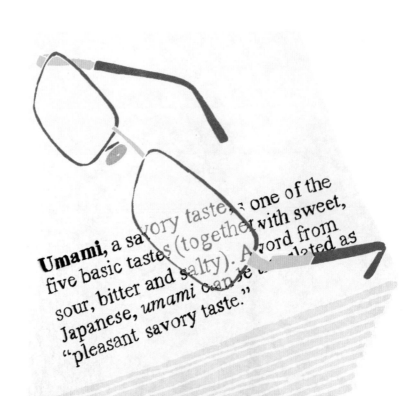

Umami, a savory taste, is one of the five basic tastes (together with sweet, sour, bitter and salty). A word from Japanese, *umami* can be translated as "pleasant savory taste."

FOOD AND CULINARY TERMS I'VE LEARNED

FRESH BASIL KEEPS BEST IN WATER
AND AT ROOM TEMPERATURE

VALUABLE COOKING TIPS

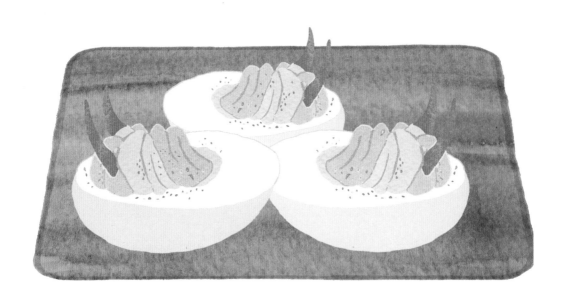

DEVILED EGGS

RECIPES I LOVE

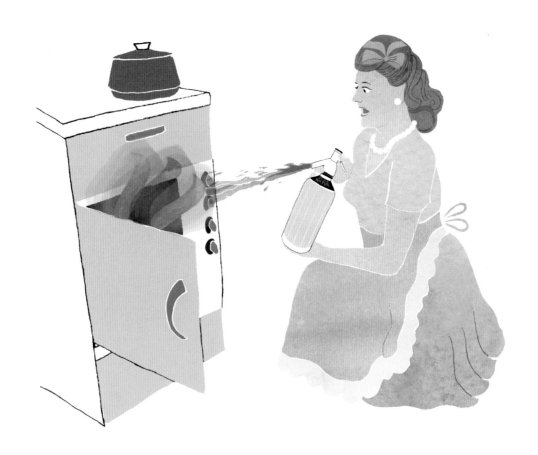

AN OVERCOOKED CASSEROLE

MY BIGGEST RECIPE FAILURES

MY DOG'S OBEDIENCE SCHOOL
GRADUATION DINNER

SPECIAL OCCASIONS I'VE COOKED FOR

POTLUCK DISHES

I'VE MADE

WANT TO MAKE

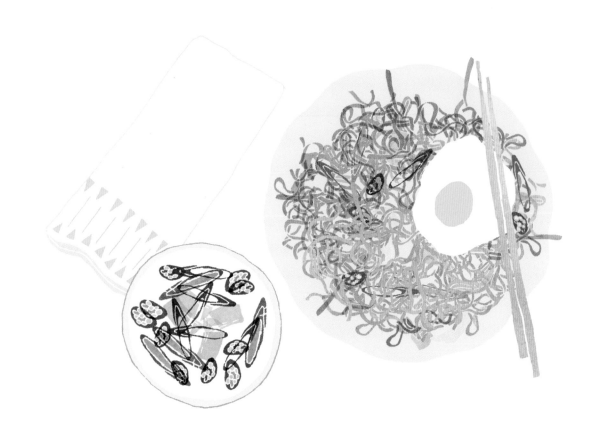

CHOW MEIN WITH LAURA IN HIGH SCHOOL

FOODS I ASSOCIATE WITH A FAMILY MEMBER OR A FRIEND

FOOD   PERSON

BRASSERIE MEURICE WITH GRANDMA

RESTAURANTS I ASSOCIATE WITH CERTAIN PEOPLE

RESTAURANT   PERSON

ADAM'S FAMOUS BBQ TOFU

FRIENDS AND FAMILY WHO HAVE COOKED FOR ME

DISH   PERSON

MEMORABLE GROCERY STORES AND GOURMET FOOD SHOPS

FOOD EVENTS, FESTIVALS, AND CULINARY ADVENTURES

I'VE ATTENDED

TO EXPLORE

CARROTS-AND-DIP TRUCK

FOOD TRUCKS AND STREET FOOD VENDORS

I'VE TRIED

WANT TO TRY

MISS GOOD LOOKIN' IS NOW A COOKIN'

SAYINGS FOR MY KITCHEN APRON

PUMPKIN PIE / FISH

FOOD AND KITCHEN SMELLS

FAVORITE   LEAST FAVORITE

ROSEMARY CLOONEY'S "MAMBO ITALIANO"

ULTIMATE DINING PLAYLIST

DINER SCENE IN *WHEN HARRY MET SALLY*

BEST FOOD-CENTRIC FILMS AND SCENES

"HOW CAN A NATION BE GREAT IF ITS BREAD
TASTES LIKE KLEENEX?" —JULIA CHILD

BEST QUOTES ABOUT FOOD

MICHAEL POLLAN'S *THE OMNIVORE'S DILEMMA*

(NON-COOKBOOK) FOOD BOOKS

I'VE READ   WANT TO READ

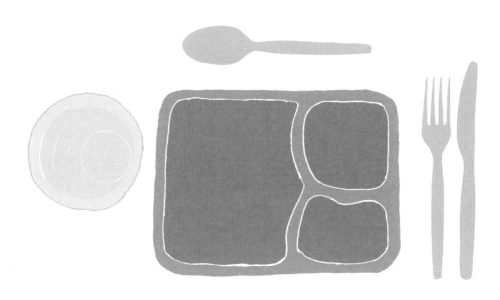

"MY LAST MEAL" FOOD LIST

MY COFFEE LIST

CAFÉ   STAR RATING

_____   ☆ ☆ ☆ ☆ ☆

_____   ☆ ☆ ☆ ☆ ☆

_____   ☆ ☆ ☆ ☆ ☆

_____   ☆ ☆ ☆ ☆ ☆

_____   ☆ ☆ ☆ ☆ ☆

_____   ☆ ☆ ☆ ☆ ☆

_____   ☆ ☆ ☆ ☆ ☆

_____   ☆ ☆ ☆ ☆ ☆

_____   ☆ ☆ ☆ ☆ ☆

_____   ☆ ☆ ☆ ☆ ☆

_____   ☆ ☆ ☆ ☆ ☆

_____   ☆ ☆ ☆ ☆ ☆

_____   ☆ ☆ ☆ ☆ ☆

_____   ☆ ☆ ☆ ☆ ☆

_____   ☆ ☆ ☆ ☆ ☆

_____   ☆ ☆ ☆ ☆ ☆

_____   ☆ ☆ ☆ ☆ ☆

_____   ☆ ☆ ☆ ☆ ☆

MY BURGER LIST

RESTAURANT	STAR RATING
	☆ ☆ ☆ ☆ ☆
	☆ ☆ ☆ ☆ ☆
	☆ ☆ ☆ ☆ ☆
	☆ ☆ ☆ ☆ ☆
	☆ ☆ ☆ ☆ ☆
	☆ ☆ ☆ ☆ ☆
	☆ ☆ ☆ ☆ ☆
	☆ ☆ ☆ ☆ ☆
	☆ ☆ ☆ ☆ ☆
	☆ ☆ ☆ ☆ ☆
	☆ ☆ ☆ ☆ ☆
	☆ ☆ ☆ ☆ ☆
	☆ ☆ ☆ ☆ ☆
	☆ ☆ ☆ ☆ ☆
	☆ ☆ ☆ ☆ ☆
	☆ ☆ ☆ ☆ ☆
	☆ ☆ ☆ ☆ ☆
	☆ ☆ ☆ ☆ ☆
	☆ ☆ ☆ ☆ ☆
	☆ ☆ ☆ ☆ ☆

MY BURRITO LIST

RESTAURANT   STAR RATING

------------------------------------   ☆ ☆ ☆ ☆ ☆

------------------------------------   ☆ ☆ ☆ ☆ ☆

------------------------------------   ☆ ☆ ☆ ☆ ☆

------------------------------------   ☆ ☆ ☆ ☆ ☆

------------------------------------   ☆ ☆ ☆ ☆ ☆

------------------------------------   ☆ ☆ ☆ ☆ ☆

------------------------------------   ☆ ☆ ☆ ☆ ☆

------------------------------------   ☆ ☆ ☆ ☆ ☆

------------------------------------   ☆ ☆ ☆ ☆ ☆

------------------------------------   ☆ ☆ ☆ ☆ ☆

------------------------------------   ☆ ☆ ☆ ☆ ☆

------------------------------------   ☆ ☆ ☆ ☆ ☆

------------------------------------   ☆ ☆ ☆ ☆ ☆

------------------------------------   ☆ ☆ ☆ ☆ ☆

------------------------------------   ☆ ☆ ☆ ☆ ☆

------------------------------------   ☆ ☆ ☆ ☆ ☆

------------------------------------   ☆ ☆ ☆ ☆ ☆

------------------------------------   ☆ ☆ ☆ ☆ ☆

------------------------------------   ☆ ☆ ☆ ☆ ☆

Baguette →

Cilantro →

Pickled carrots
& Radishes →

Tofu →

Cucumber →

Jalapeño →

Mayonnaise →

MY SANDWICH LIST

RESTAURANT   STAR RATING

---------------------------------------   ☆ ☆ ☆ ☆ ☆

---------------------------------------   ☆ ☆ ☆ ☆ ☆

---------------------------------------   ☆ ☆ ☆ ☆ ☆

---------------------------------------   ☆ ☆ ☆ ☆ ☆

---------------------------------------   ☆ ☆ ☆ ☆ ☆

---------------------------------------   ☆ ☆ ☆ ☆ ☆

---------------------------------------   ☆ ☆ ☆ ☆ ☆

---------------------------------------   ☆ ☆ ☆ ☆ ☆

---------------------------------------   ☆ ☆ ☆ ☆ ☆

---------------------------------------   ☆ ☆ ☆ ☆ ☆

---------------------------------------   ☆ ☆ ☆ ☆ ☆

---------------------------------------   ☆ ☆ ☆ ☆ ☆

---------------------------------------   ☆ ☆ ☆ ☆ ☆

---------------------------------------   ☆ ☆ ☆ ☆ ☆

---------------------------------------   ☆ ☆ ☆ ☆ ☆

---------------------------------------   ☆ ☆ ☆ ☆ ☆

---------------------------------------   ☆ ☆ ☆ ☆ ☆

---------------------------------------   ☆ ☆ ☆ ☆ ☆

MY PIZZA LIST

RESTAURANT	STAR RATING
------------------------------	☆ ☆ ☆ ☆ ☆
------------------------------	☆ ☆ ☆ ☆ ☆
------------------------------	☆ ☆ ☆ ☆ ☆
------------------------------	☆ ☆ ☆ ☆ ☆
------------------------------	☆ ☆ ☆ ☆ ☆
------------------------------	☆ ☆ ☆ ☆ ☆
------------------------------	☆ ☆ ☆ ☆ ☆
------------------------------	☆ ☆ ☆ ☆ ☆
------------------------------	☆ ☆ ☆ ☆ ☆
------------------------------	☆ ☆ ☆ ☆ ☆
------------------------------	☆ ☆ ☆ ☆ ☆
------------------------------	☆ ☆ ☆ ☆ ☆
------------------------------	☆ ☆ ☆ ☆ ☆
------------------------------	☆ ☆ ☆ ☆ ☆
------------------------------	☆ ☆ ☆ ☆ ☆
------------------------------	☆ ☆ ☆ ☆ ☆
------------------------------	☆ ☆ ☆ ☆ ☆
------------------------------	☆ ☆ ☆ ☆ ☆
------------------------------	☆ ☆ ☆ ☆ ☆

DRAW HERE

MY _____ LIST

RESTAURANT	STAR RATING
--	☆ ☆ ☆ ☆ ☆
--	☆ ☆ ☆ ☆ ☆
--	☆ ☆ ☆ ☆ ☆
--	☆ ☆ ☆ ☆ ☆
--	☆ ☆ ☆ ☆ ☆
--	☆ ☆ ☆ ☆ ☆
--	☆ ☆ ☆ ☆ ☆
--	☆ ☆ ☆ ☆ ☆
--	☆ ☆ ☆ ☆ ☆
--	☆ ☆ ☆ ☆ ☆
--	☆ ☆ ☆ ☆ ☆
--	☆ ☆ ☆ ☆ ☆
--	☆ ☆ ☆ ☆ ☆
--	☆ ☆ ☆ ☆ ☆
--	☆ ☆ ☆ ☆ ☆
--	☆ ☆ ☆ ☆ ☆
--	☆ ☆ ☆ ☆ ☆
--	☆ ☆ ☆ ☆ ☆
--	☆ ☆ ☆ ☆ ☆
--	☆ ☆ ☆ ☆ ☆

DRAW HERE

MY _____ LIST

RESTAURANT	STAR RATING
----------------------------	☆ ☆ ☆ ☆ ☆
----------------------------	☆ ☆ ☆ ☆ ☆
----------------------------	☆ ☆ ☆ ☆ ☆
----------------------------	☆ ☆ ☆ ☆ ☆
----------------------------	☆ ☆ ☆ ☆ ☆
----------------------------	☆ ☆ ☆ ☆ ☆
----------------------------	☆ ☆ ☆ ☆ ☆
----------------------------	☆ ☆ ☆ ☆ ☆
----------------------------	☆ ☆ ☆ ☆ ☆
----------------------------	☆ ☆ ☆ ☆ ☆
----------------------------	☆ ☆ ☆ ☆ ☆
----------------------------	☆ ☆ ☆ ☆ ☆
----------------------------	☆ ☆ ☆ ☆ ☆
----------------------------	☆ ☆ ☆ ☆ ☆
----------------------------	☆ ☆ ☆ ☆ ☆
----------------------------	☆ ☆ ☆ ☆ ☆
----------------------------	☆ ☆ ☆ ☆ ☆
----------------------------	☆ ☆ ☆ ☆ ☆
----------------------------	☆ ☆ ☆ ☆ ☆
----------------------------	☆ ☆ ☆ ☆ ☆

FAVORITE RESTAURANTS BY CUISINE

CUISINE   RESTAURANT

FAVORITE RESTAURANTS BY CUISINE

CUISINE   RESTAURANT

FAVORITE RESTAURANTS BY CUISINE

CUISINE   RESTAURANT

SELLING LEMONADE, SUMMER, 5TH GRADE

FOOD-RELATED MEMORIES

EATING HOMEGROWN FOOD ON MY FRIEND'S FARM

MOST MEMORABLE MEALS

THE *SEINFELD* TV SHOW RESTAURANT

RESTAURANTS TO TRY

- [ ] _____
- [ ] _____
- [ ] _____
- [ ] _____
- [ ] _____
- [ ] _____
- [ ] _____
- [ ] _____
- [ ] _____
- [ ] _____
- [ ] _____
- [ ] _____
- [ ] _____
- [ ] _____
- [ ] _____
- [ ] _____
- [ ] _____
- [ ] _____
- [ ] _____

RESTAURANTS TO TRY

- [ ] _____
- [ ] _____
- [ ] _____
- [ ] _____
- [ ] _____
- [ ] _____
- [ ] _____
- [ ] _____
- [ ] _____
- [ ] _____
- [ ] _____
- [ ] _____
- [ ] _____
- [ ] _____
- [ ] _____
- [ ] _____
- [ ] _____
- [ ] _____
- [ ] _____
- [ ] _____

RESTAURANTS TO TRY

☐ --

☐ --

☐ --

☐ --

☐ --

☐ --

☐ --

☐ --

☐ --

☐ --

☐ --

☐ --

☐ --

☐ --

☐ --

☐ --

☐ --

☐ --

☐ --

☐ --

RESTAURANTS TO TRY

- [ ]
- [ ]
- [ ]
- [ ]
- [ ]
- [ ]
- [ ]
- [ ]
- [ ]
- [ ]
- [ ]
- [ ]
- [ ]
- [ ]
- [ ]
- [ ]
- [ ]
- [ ]
- [ ]
- [ ]

RESTAURANTS TO TRY

- [ ] --
- [ ] --
- [ ] --
- [ ] --
- [ ] --
- [ ] --
- [ ] --
- [ ] --
- [ ] --
- [ ] --
- [ ] --
- [ ] --
- [ ] --
- [ ] --
- [ ] --
- [ ] --
- [ ] --
- [ ] --
- [ ] --
- [ ] --

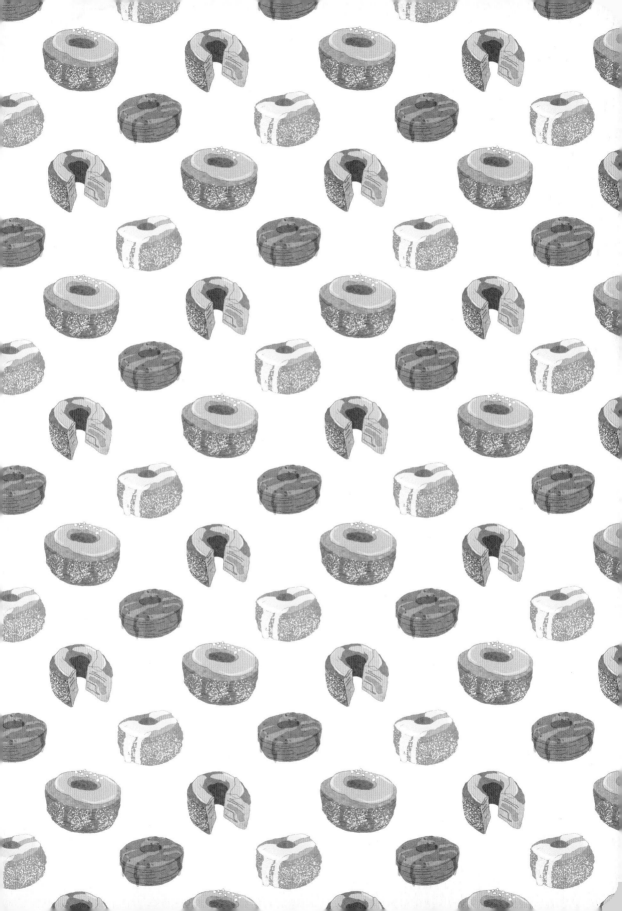

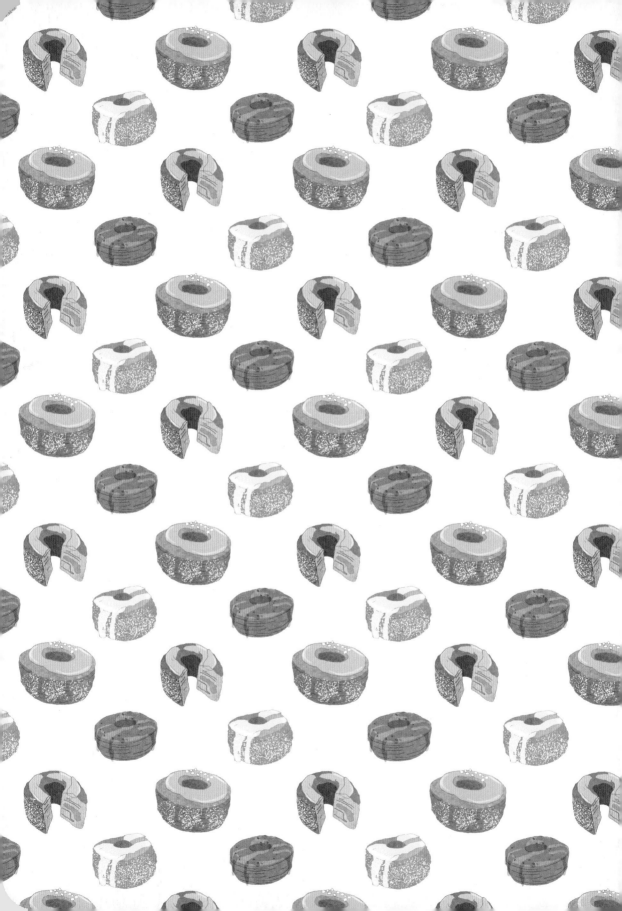